UNBECOMING BEHAVIOR

KATE COLBY

UGLY DUCKLING PRESSE

BROOKLYN | 2008

for
Todd Shalom

For God's sake, a ship leaving port
is still a wonderful thing to see.

—JANE BOWLES
[from *Two Serious Ladies*]

Mornings grow slowly
from the ground up

pinched-off
balls of meat are
rolling from the bowl
they are
meatballs

they are
writing postcards, stacks
of little thumbing snaps
at the lips of public tables

lick, slap, go
the ladies
three down and still
they are
utterly delightful.

Warm light cuts cold
triangles from parapets

carpet-beat
halos
radiating motes minarets of blue
ululation you are

running like a knife
through pats for toasting
exacting breakfasts
where stubborn delicacies
still taste like their recipes.

I can't go everywhere, be everything.
Every day a new balloon.
I'm blowing up into bunches.

To be xenophobic about one's own history;
I meant it then, but look at me now, puffy
sleeves plumped and wry for the revival.

Her infinite mantel
of curio ships
outgrowing their bottles like last-ditch participants
in historic love affairs—

Cherifa is stacking the dishes.
Untouched tea and toast are infuriating.

—or victims
of high-profile disasters.

The suffering donkeys, the sound
of fronds. The smell of small fires.
The heart is never at home, only
pushing through, so nothing draws
a bead on you.

A breathing heart beating
into the starting line,
a tacking pack of red flags
wooing the committee boat
of inflatable marks *bang*

false starts get you
seven-twenty
circles jerking
around yourself.

•

A grand circle of the arm and hand
ends cupped around a stage whisper,
Miss Marion reads Rabelais.

The townspeople go wild
—beat—
now talk amongst yourselves

cabbages and rutabagas
cabbages and rutabagas

She's a real character, meaning
having crossed the line of method-
acted methods of relation

a collective case
of stage rage:
give pause, get
over yourself.

Beside herself with stagy gestures
of indecision, knowing the moment
the mind is made it inches out
in front of you

to get ahead
of yourself

Don't be that guy, my brother
says to everyone else on the road.

He's all over the road

over the road

repeating till there's no

meaning, meaning

Masshole.

The poorest places
are always painted
the nicest shades of sherbet

surprise surprise

There are methods all over the map.

•

To latch on, like a baby,
is what it takes (to take
to) each time. To nudge
around and find a nipple.

One later tries to cut the futzing
(unless it's where your mouth is.)

When Jane tries to write she feels the desert in her mouth, a not-unpleasant taste of old parchment. And preserved lemon. Her selfish idea of character development only exists in the fourth dimension—slices of life circle like bored wagon wheels. They fall in tinny crescendos, something like a rabbit's death scream. Something like candied peels. Or reception sticks. Old-fashioned confections whose subtlety does not suit contemporary life.

write through it, goes the old line, stick it
out, as though a life were a weak filament
shedding nothing over anything, but necessary
to keep buzzing, anyway

A stale motel room with a slippery synthetic coverlet.

The rangy nineteen-year-old handyman who only got his pants half-off before the show was over.

Back at the ranch, the dudes with new boots and feet up in front of the lodge. Chops locked in reflexive drawl. The horse doctor was kicked in the jaw, displaced it by four inches.

We are both afraid of horses. For one thing.

We who squeeze
our knees
against jerks.

•

The ladies always
write the postcards
neat white notes
in rows
like prayer flags
they are shredding on the wind

events not given
to repetition

making good time
immemorial

The higher the odds are stacked
against them
the more columnar they become

Witness:
an eclipse, awakening
thirty years of deep sleep.

What else is under your belt.

Stabbing at the Atlas is how
we wound up in a tin can, tail-
gating a listing van of bugging
parcels, top-
heavy with hog-tied sheep atop the roof rack.

Toddlers are pushed
into hairpins, hawking
faceted rocks, geodesic
mirrors. Each is unique.

The fumes have gone to our heads.

We have gone to our heads.

Spent the night at Aït Benhaddou.

Beer was made available
in the Barbary
reception tent.

Next morning we were stuck
in the desert. Didn't know
to choke the engine.

(This has been written
down, is all
I remember.)

(I am my own strongest alloy
of calculated risks
racked against a precious ore.)

That night, the shifty stars, distant
candles flickered in the casbah.
R was upstairs, asleep under seven
rough blankets, I have never been
so decomposed, rather one very self-
same thing.

Must consolidate our messaging.

Lump it. says Jane, wants to do
just one thing in her life.
Prefers grazing
sheep to a sweeping vista.

Every dusting takes the edge off.

She's a real, dyed-in-the-wool
preference for stocking seams,
runs.

•

Triangulate from every point
to divine the solar plexus.

Or build a trussed
span, but infinitely;
how else
to support the center.

Begin again with prickly
heat, an elbow hickey,
eczema that festers
in the pliant places

excess skin grows sticky
with accommodated movement

positively phototropic

The summer I was seven, the gypsy
moths infested, caterpillars wriggled
from the sky, tangled in my ratty
hair, formed knots, crawling skin,
shivers, peristaltic on the sidewalk.

With sticks we ripped the spun
tents from tree forks, exposed
knots of seething, pimpling
pupae.

Hackled and shuddering
with silverfish, fly spit,
a childhood is itchy
and now
standing on its end.

Stinging nettles, tiny hairs
of hooked skin, throwing
burrs at others' backs, sticks,
stabbing through your thin shirt

hives buzz
at night induced
by heat pocked skin
throbbing cicadas
shrieking bites
the night the glowing

bug zapper

My sticky nightie, this itching
keeps me awake, can't get
away with myself

—not here, in temperate
Western clime, where I am no-
body has gone to my head

[I am]

negatively geotropic

Caterpillars gather periodically,
climb to the tips of branches
and dangle from silk threads,
catch the wind to a new location
in a practice called "ballooning."

•

Jane refuses *majoun*
lest things begin to flicker
in the corner of the eye,
to rustle in the curtains.

Her skin is perforable
like tin, to let nebulae
shine through, but new
formations she doesn't need,
prefers to keep the flimsy
surface sealed.

The ceiling spins
with the merely
observable. Inside-
out. No matter.

No wormholes
or paths in her plots, plants
them in with patchy hedges.
(Loathes the scrolling
sanctums of the Loire.)

Jane sunbathes on the roof
behind an incandescent parapet.

Concentrated light and heat
give pressure, pinch
and seal her off inside,
drawing from her head

half-formed thoughts
curl up like bits of dry parchment

she'll feed her own furnace.

What I am stoking with what
comes to mind: stars
on the ceiling of Grand Central,
age ten—punching tin
at Plymouth Plantation,

rinky-dink lamps for bedside tables.

Her eyes are like fan blades
straining against the ceiling.

•

Jane was fifteen when thrown
from a horse, contracted
TB of the knee. Spent
two years in traction

suspended in a medium
of herself, slurry
of pulling skin
and flesh against bone

cribbed and confined
in contempt of expectation;
white walls, a whistling
radiator and bed rail.

(This is easy.)

Once I had a breast lump
had to wait two weeks
have never been
so relieved.

This play is titled WYSIWYG
or the delay
in our prognoses

to be entirely self-contained

I'll watch my own narrow back.

•

Unpack your acronyms.

And decant yourself.

Are you in or out?

Our suspended particulates
I'm inter-filtering, effecting
a flickering lucidity as in
dementia: the spirographic
necessity of empty centers.

To be a satellite of galaxies

burning to always
only make do.

Toward the cold glow
of the Revo we drew
chairs to the window,
drank from the bottle.

Outside, bathed in border light,
the made-up women of the night.

In conjectural Meso-
american ball games
the winner is sacrificed
to save the sun.

•

Jane is tapping
imaginary ashes

    over the railing
    stirred
    by fricative fronds,
    the whited-out light

awash in the always
seasonable weather.

                Warm northern winters, cold
                Pacific summers, incongruous
                weather events are depressing

                    (let's remain
                    in that rut, tar baby; see what sticks.)

                Let that hat wear you, and them
                come to you. May it always be
                your stunning debut—where it ends
                you begin. Stay out of the wings
                and the will-call.

There's a one-track practice
of mining the mind, with thought-
trains unwired to self-terrorize.

                Suspicious cells
get caught in corners and pulse

fruitlessly, like Christmas
bulbs, neon
signs on the fritz

dead-end games
of artificial life.

You pinch yourself off,
interbreed, cannibalize
and survive

in this case, from filling station
to filling station.

Curl up and begin
again, blow up and across
the border like tumbleweeds.
Scattering seeds.

Upstream the anglers stand shoulder-to-shoulder.

•

Cannibalizing my own
cast-off poems, I am
the mother of necessity

repurposing rusty
hooks and lines,
my fair-weather
faux amis.

Terrain changes
but the short-cuts remain,
like wormholes, the lines
I should cut them, but let
them swallow me.
                Fine.
                My guest.
                Be my own home.

        Hardwired with strings
        of bulbs on the blink or gone
        haywire, imprinting the night
        violet traces of light
        through tin or gnats or picked
        scabs. Now what's eating me.

        Veneers are vulnerable at Christmas.

Jane flees the seaside
palapa for Taxco,
where the hills have been
blessedly hollowed
of silver.

Can't stop counting
the waves, her heart
through the night
pounding, broken
sea, washes
plots and potential
breakfast menus.

Can't crack
this bloody
habit, like desert flora
I poison my seedlings,   the pipes
(the pipes)
the squeak
of wipers, bloody
handprints at the Motel 6

what's doing
a girl like you
in on a night like this.

Can't stop counting
the stairs I climb,
thought breaks
over, begin
again.
One.
Disbelieves in going backwards.

Catching myself in the act—

The thatch scratches in the breeze.
He's typing.
She's counting.
Imagines it's involuntary.

In Taxco there's a fine layer of dust.
Bright walls grown
dingy with local color
of WPA murals.

•

Expats equal expats
at the pukka cantina

Belly up to their own
prelapsarian reflections,
steamship labels, crushed
linen, pithy hats,
prefer a mirror to a mirador

the soi-disant auto-
didacts, unwittingly
living on ruins.

Raise up your
swizzle sticks, citizens—
join the march

the way the studio becomes the art.

•

Hayfoot,
meet Strawfoot
and a bona fide
Los Banos taco

belly-full of Pea Soup
Andersen's, I've died
countless I-5 suicides.

Plan B: wind yourself
like a stripe
to a pole, to have been
driven to distraction
    I
my ranch and aqueduct
my smell of offal
my blood

being drawn by a corrugated border.

Some things are only true in fiction;   be true to yourself!
say,
    tell them you're from Boston,
    and they'll chalk you up a class
    act. Your ducky dockside dad
    in a deathless madras jacket.

    How to out-do what happens
    to be true. To be cancelled.

        Crest, meet trough,
        I am nothing if not
        oyster crackers.

Jane is gay, lame, Jewish;
I am a drawer full of golf pencils.
Coasters. We collapse, become
singular and are full of ourselves.

Smoldering starlets, all
goo-goo-eyed, cooing
at our own reflections,
flinging elliptical
air kisses.

I've a thing for entitled urchins
racing their faces, in dead-
heat with incongruous graces
and expertly letting out wick.

Becky, Lily, Carrie—
like watching a train
wreck, wouldn't I
do the same?

To be dependent, determined
by wealth and weather, object
of Naturalist voodoo:

what's coming to you.

Jane is thinking the unthinkable.

We are beggars
of exception, be it
local or thruway,
P.S. or country day

Eating deviled
ham from the can
at any rate
we are
slumming it.

•

Seeing myself
in the corner
of my eye

harp tucked
in the crook
of my arm, crown
digging into temples.

I am Beauty incarnate,
as frozen in stone-
cold parish hall,
cutis erectus in the footlights.

Gobo hearts rotate.
Creaky chairs reclaim
their folds

this false
attribution
of feeling

Your prepossessed hearts
being won by the dozen—please
take me for my body
double

in dreams
I understudy
others' eyes.

Dear Jane,
would that
I could see you.

Plan C—must consume
ourselves with ourselves.

But Jane can't stand
still like that, instead
milks her hard-won
jolie-laide, forgoing
feathers for a fright wig.

A practiced natural,
sideshow shoo-in,
squandered prodigy
or idiot savant

exactingly prodigal,
unsparing
with cold cream

We are
nature morte,
tableau vivant.

•

Catching
myself in the act

rummaging for ready-made
things I've already thought
and never want to think again.

oo, see what I said? Now stick it
in the back of the curio cabinet.

Exhibit A: Control V

(here goes nothing.)

:

Tessellated light through a dozen
closing doors, and day breaks
on Merzouga. The trite light of
epiphany; they've taken her head

being consumed by her own

drapery, our Venus
rent with cracks.

•

What is learned, rote
with repetition

say it
over again
and all is not

not the info, rather
the category
it falls into

things that ring
false, like similes

reconstructed memories

dead as arrival
and a little more so
every time.

The hazards of certain
occupations: pressing
heat and braziers' haze
over the Djemaa el Fna.
Punched tin and tooled
leather. Tennis elbow.

Sixty years of
soot in the lungs, collapsing
mendicants, acrobats, alms,
palm-frond donkeys
that dry and crumble
with the circular words
of the wizened.

Sixty years itinerant,
his overturned bucket.
His sixty-first time telling
the tenth Arabian Night.

This is the dying tradition.

Canned
calls to prayer
are rolling through the square
the staticky minarets.

Jane trades in on fey ladies
blurry faces on stationary
trains, tracked to Point B
and so on or back again.

In no danger of being
anthologized, her slow
self-serving self-
suicide. A personal
pact and spit-shake.

Her drops of dye in water
that disperse or become
muddy with the other
colors. Her other lives
even less remarkable.

Point B:
How often did Grandma recall
him ditching his car and walking home
from Boston to Wellesley in driving snow
with a bag of lobsters for dinner.

Maybe five.   (Who would do that?)

I never knew my great-grandfather,
nor his like, for the love of which
she repeatedly told me this story.

•

Now ten years Californian
and no longer in relief.
A thin skin wound
around this coast, my one-
time choke-hold

becoming symbiotic
negatively synergetic.

How is new memory different from old?

am I
more or less
more or less
my edges
being beveled

With time I want to dance
again, again
become
the ballerina I almost was

now I'm combined,
cooked and collapsed,
no longer read like a pop-up book.

No longer lady-
like, I'm coming into
unbecoming behavior

must keep one
leg shaking
under the table

Primped in periphery
of three-way mirrors
can't be-
hold myself
head-on
frozen
my own headlights.

My own breakdowns
in transit as counter
to stylized advantages of the road
movie

melt down and take on

my container
the lay of the land (we are all in it.)

Stuck in sand
a thousand miles from the border

out of gas, rocks
embedded in the undercarriage

dings, dust, blood
shot with radiator water.

Cataviña ninety-eight
boojums bend among the boulders.

We are going to bury something
or dig it up, find
or lose ourselves.

Synchronic mental
geocache, synaptic
X's in invisible ink

about face
and count
backwards.

Death Valley oh-six. Dirty
salt pan, saltated sand and
surface creep

articulate tent poles
through terrible night
wind of speed
train tunneling
end to end

night night

and dead
morning's
clastic strata

It's all uphill from here.

Jane wears herself
like fire retardant,
the peeling bark
of certain self-
preserving trees

as broken contrails contain the desert.

Her plume de nom
dissolving, breaking
down into barbicels

reticulated flights
of fancy into walls,
doors slam, deflate
soufflés, gasps
leave the splattered
to the sidewalk.

I'm wheezing in the wee-est
hours, membranes
seized in dreams
of alleyways

someone is cupping
the side of your head,
behind the ear, fingers

jingle of mariachi pants,
itinerant musicians.

•

Jane's stuck on island
time, circling
girdling seaboard

round the clock
the sea

wading
light, salt
white
washed
out, un-
sightly
squinting
and over-
exposed.

A pustule of palms
he's bought to boil
down, reduce
or render, maybe
his own gravy.

Ceylon, Ceylon—

or lap around
yourself, close
spiders weaving
squeaming
sea things
bottom feeding
wishy
washing
in and out.

Twilit fruit
bats swoop
into mangoes
into rubbery
wings they
tuck and roost
upended

—appending again
in fits and false starts
the horizon at hand:
spiny rambutans,
Kasemsan, no, Tonga

two-thousand
dusky bats descend
over dinner.
Tinny beef
in hollows of green
paw-paws, broken

pallet   night, sweat
slept with my foot
against the net

By morning it was sucked
dry, swollen to twice its

burnished skin
of pure itching
hollow thrumming
waves on beveled
edges, red
sun of sailors
says warning:
morning, soggy
Wheetabix.

Mango juice pooling
in your elbow, toe
jam. Fruiting bodies
of something fungal.

The slow sound of creaking
ropes, sighs, torpid fans

est-ce que
parce que

Elbow grease, filthy
shards of soap.

A thin skin of tumid heat,
hair, sweated rings
on faded tables of teak, salt
air, un-
crystalline and creeping.

Jane spends her days wading
tepid rings to forestall the salt.
In slow circles swelling, over-
stepping soft purple stars,
pulpy jelly-things and sea slugs.

At night, the devil
dancing on the mainland

from his stilted pavilion
of sputtering hurricanes

knick-knack exotica,
spiny urchins
dried and rendered
delicate by the sun

(reflecting)

my fine lines
around the eyes
my photo-
pigmentation.

Pigs snout in cemeteries
of fluttering plastic, broken
bottles. I was running with
fists full of rocks, faked-out
horrible dogs at my ankles

rabbity piglets nosing for holes
in the matted vegetation.

Pigs root for remnants,
nudging clams at low tide,
squealing in perpetual death
screams, naked, pink-eyed,
wrapped and rendered
in leaves for underground ovens.

(offset, these machinated
mises en abîme)

(you've made up your mind
now, lie in it.)

Outside a ring
of mosquito
coils
the palpable hum
of the periphery.

Small bodies
are caught
in orbit netted: future
husband

fetid
honey bucket crackling
palmettos

Jane in her unmentionables

contracting
island
fever.

•

My resistance to the lures
of lobster buoys

extant rustic
signals

dites-
moi pourquoi

I'd prop them in the corner.

My bent of dis-
mantling syntagms
like sticky buns

decanting them back
into ingredients

Fluttering fingers of *Für*
Elise, practiced sight
reading table-
mannered teen

soft salt light of
choked-up put-puts, dead
heat, thighs
stuck to seat

and sickly
smell of privet
rotting picket
tinny wicket
ring around the
Cape-shaped house

(among the nasty
habits I practice
simply because I know how.)

—over here, futzing
at the end of the keyboard,
while the business is carried
out in the bass notes.

Must keep moving,
always letting
left hand know
what right hand's doing.

Which fork
and in what order
what to pour
in your crystal snifter.

What rests on my linens,
Waterford and willowware.
Claw picks. Hang dinner,
I'm only in it for the trivets

drawn to the blue
pulse at the center
of the votive.

Small bodies are caught in orbit,
space debris,
drawn only by their memories,
have absented themselves, say,
we defectors from other fishbowls.

—cut, cue curtain
and back
to what's after
these messages
(building my brand
of historic invention.)

Jim Thompson was
(this time,
this world)
a man's man, self-
made in his image,
clipped head,
wings to the war,
ballooned to another
set, take
or *mise*
en scène.

In the grip of his ripcord,
a fruiting spore
from another culture's incubator.

Spread his mind
all over matter,
to wing it and carry
the sky to the water,
a would-be kingdom
come by counting

back: ten
clap, take
two. stop.

say,
who packed your parachute?

Dangling from silk threads—

all of Bangkok
all of Bangkok

and rooted there: Soi
Kasemsan on the klong
his stilted teak
house eked
from cast-offs of other
more intact traditions.

His soi disant
soie changeant
reflexive slubs
or imperfections twisted
into something marketable.

The hot smell of fruiting
peels, feeble fires, all
wrists and fingers

dancers lean and shuffle
around reclining
Buddha's spiny headgear.

Consider yourself
at home on the boards
of others' has-been habitations

rattling *tuk-tuks*
trickling sounds
of sonic coagulants
so that
you can see the heat
in the whited light
through the cracks
in the walls and shutters.

The point: to be
the flame they circle
blue and gyroscopic
shape of his relations

at the eye of their attention,
till you start to walk
like being watched
by the eyes in the back
of your own head
and there's no one there to see it.

Be the music
while the music lasts—

or pull a disappearing act

before the delicate
cocoon is destroyed
by the itchy occupant
secreting its way out.

Say, philology leads
to calamity—stop,
stab student,
flop into wingchair

a cloud of powder
comes forth from my hair.

pause
here
and gather
your character
consider yourself
come into your own
thin skin
glowering
at the guts

And the audience goes wild
for my all-out meltdown
in make-up, patrician talc
and apothecary laugh lines.

collect yourself
and count
to ten
my ribs

I am dripping
in the lights. this is
to be twice removed
and easy
to get a rise
despite the dried-up
yolk rattling
around inside
the smooth
white
shell.

•

Jane makes a home within
warm red walls, pulsing
heart of the Medina

a stooping
sort of
stuck in the world

perennial snow
day depending

globe-bound
boughs bending

against the pane *(I like the rain.)*

insistent
difference
in and out

Our staticky prayer
of imminent closure
broadcast: digging
in, down,
heavy

Jane is getting closer. Musty
rugs reek of resin from the Rif,
thick steam, tagine of gamy
pigeon, raisins, wadded paper,
cotton swabs and sweaty walls

exhausted bottles
unlikely ladies
collective kefta
meatballs.

Frail skins scud
across the rug
every time
the door is opened   they are livid
withered
roses.

Jane's got a wen, has let
herself go with a snap
of underpants elastic.

Cherifa is practicing
magic, with packets
of fingernails around
the incubating house

revanche   and
watch your elbows

soupçons   sloshing
in with cupped ears

(another paper fan
I'm folding into
its own vacant spaces)

Jane no longer believes in creation,
only compromised containers
she'll reinforce as needed.

To be digestive, self-
secreting, bottom-feeding
her own geotropic bottom.

Consumes herself with herself, self-
self-administration—like haroset
dense and dull
but dense
with indehiscent nuts.

The curse is reversed.

To be the bowl of the sky
looking in at its own
ruminated guts.

There are no decisions
to be made, a sickness
comes at her with a skinny needle
wheedling

You won't feel a thing.

(Must consolidate our messaging.)

"At night, the blue *djenoun* curl among the mountains
and swallows no longer fly above the city."

"They cover their heads
and wait to be swallowed."

•

Begin again and forgive
another intervention
(on-message, but counter
to customer retention.)

Consider yourself
at home in this poem, pounding
through the night, in her head
they keep up the construction—
a preemptive network of unmade beds

a different one of each in which
she spends each outward-reaching night

a different guest unmade to feel
at home away from which
she neither makes nor helps
herself to absolutely everything.

Are you lost
yet
in syntactic gymnastics
(another of those
nasty habits
I earlier referred to)

Her home is forever
ad interim, her medium
says summon
the sound
of chattering
teeth, missing
keys
mouthy sounds
in one's own head.

(I hear my haunted
organs singing.)

Breathless specters
caught in corners

pulsing self-
contentedly

with what you'd just
as soon or rather later
rather never see.

Ghosts moan in the sexy spaces
under the stairs and bulging
gables,
swing from the severed sash cords
of peculiar interior windows.

She's neither plan nor process;
the windows shift,
but not the prospect

hair-colored hills with knots
of dingy sheep, harrowing
dust and dusty birds
unrelieved against it.

If she stops building she will die
or more likely disappear
from the corner of her eye.

This is the wild Winchester
widow of the West—

another of the slapped-
together backdrops
to which
I've not adapted still
stalled
on each
saltating
particulate.

But here, for the moment
I am building a home
for my branching family
cellular progeny
of every splitting second.

Home is where your hand is
madly waving in front of your face
and whether you can see it.

The unsightly can't be seen
through the sight of the bead
on your own
furrowing
forehead.

a gnash of waxy Dracula teeth

to want to die
in someone else's sleep

vis à vis à vis à vis

•

To be a source, not cause
effective sign says no
wake, so they sleep
centuries in the summer house.

Must pinch ourselves
off, hang
flag and salute our past
with what we've got to work with

the tournament tree and registry

among the things I'm ashamed of

how fireworks make me cry
how the ship is shrinking
in its bottle, will turn to dust
leaving only the container
which everyone will see
and nobody will register.

What will be
will be
as long as it moves so slowly
it leaves no smack of wake
among the color-coded
lobster buoys.

Mildew grows slowly,
from the ground up

walls, sails,
salty towels, around
the bottom of your teacup.

We don't see the unsightly
crumbling mullions,
broken sash cords slack
beside the windows that
rattle in their casements
when the weather turns

at night
shades
whack
and suck against the screens.

This is the summer house,
our swelling sea, our bailers,
the rice in the shakers,
mildew metastasizes
through the mattresses,
mismatched linens, fingering
up the plastic shower curtains.

The windows warp, but not
the vantage, crab grass
creeps about the castle, keep
eyes fixed so as not to see it

our ocular
aphasia

our bulging blue
hydrangeas.

This is the summer house
of bedsteads peeling
in prelapsarian parsimony
whose itchy inhabitants
adeptly practice adaptation.

What doesn't kill you
doesn't kill you
hence, the mildew

our deathless
motif
number one.

•

My kingdom has come
of age inside the ugly
contemporary church

my historical society's
favorite eyesore

my favorite pew

in the stained light
straining through

a fruitless, afforded
chance at perfection

keeps me a little
rough around the edges.

My wobbly aria
my rhyme-y pastiche
of personal first
parish of all
for one
and one
for
all
or or
for
nothing nothing

doing all we're in for.

I am neither
ecumenical
nor meant
for this world.

The ladies are running
lists and newsy letters

my historical romance
my Fruitlands
my plantation
as settlement

salting, dipping,
churning, carding,
lumpy pan-
dowdy, slump
and fool

Jane is now
homemaker,
an empty nest

with time

to spackle paint the pool.

•

Like nails through the weight-
bearing elements of your home
can anything be pounded in?

To answer, again, with fuzzy
gray grid-dots at interstices
of a favorite optical illusion

say, the way crouching felines
fade into the matted forest.

Jane curls up
like a cellophane
fish in the palm
of an unseen hand

dreams of amniotic
woods and words
that can almost do

the same

repeating

there's no meaning

an unmarked grave

a preemptive reading

the small army you are feeding

                    a drawing room
                    full of women
                    watching the door

What is rolled
between the palms
until perfectly
symmetrical.

NOTES

page 39

"...the music while the music lasts," from T.S. Eliot, "Four Quartets."

page 40

"Philology leads to calamity." from Eugène Ionesco, *The Lesson*, 1951.

page 45

Quotations from Paul Bowles, *Points in Time*, Ecco Press, 1982 and Kate Colby, "Pangaea Redivivus / Re[as]sembling Anastasia," *Fruitlands*, Litmus Press, 2006.